Lynr
in ass(
for

The world premiere

Returning to Haifa

by

Ghassan Kanafani

adapted by

Ismail Khalidi and Naomi Wallace

FINBOROUGH | THEATRE

FINBOROUGH | THEATRE

First performed at the Finborough Theatre
27 February 2018

RETURNING TO HAIFA

by Ghassan Kanafani
adapted by Ismail Khalidi and Naomi Wallace

Said	**Ammar Haj Ahmad**
Safiyya	**Myriam Acharki**
Young Safiyya	**Leila Ayad**
Young Said/Dov	**Ethan Kai**
Miriam	**Marlene Sidaway**

Director	**Caitlin McLeod**
Set and Costume Designer	**Rosie Elnile**
Lighting Designer	**Joshua Gadsby**
Sound Designer	**David Gregory**
Movement Director	**Lanre Malaolu**
Casting Director	**Arthur Carrington**
Stage Manager	**Amy Whitby-Baker**
Production Manager	**Ben Karakashian**
Producer	**Lynne McConway**
Production Assistant	**Valentina Behrouzi**

Ramallah and Haifa and the road in between.
1947, 1948 and 1967.

The performance lasts approximately eighty minutes.

There will be no interval.

Supported using public funding by
**ARTS COUNCIL
ENGLAND**

Our patrons are respectfully reminded that, in this intimate theatre, any noise such as rustling programmes, talking or the ringing of mobile phones may distract the actors and your fellow audience-members.

We regret there is no admittance or re-admittance to the auditorium whilst the performance is in progress.

Myriam Acharki | Saffiya

Theatre includes *Kabeirol* (Punchdrunk), *Dionysos Unbound* (Bridewell Theatre), *Jane Eyre* (West End and Tour for Shared Experience), *Woyzeck* (St Ann's Warehouse, New York City and Gate Theatre), *The Seven Year Itch* (Queen's Theatre), *Macbeth False Memory* (Actors Touring Company), *Princess Sharon* (Scarlet Theatre) and *Peter Pan* (West Yorkshire Playhouse).

Film includes *City of Tiny Lights*, *28 K*, *John Carter of Mars* and *The Beach*.

Television includes *Next of Kin*, *Doctors*, *Chasing Shadows*, *Silk*, *Sinbad*, *New Tricks*, *E20*, *Under Suspicion*, *Little Miss Jocelyn*, *Human Cargo*, *Paradise Heights* and *Holby City*.

Leila Ayad | Young Safiyya

Trained at Rose Bruford College.

Theatre includes *Elton John's Glasses* (Palace Theatre, Watford) and *Imogen* (Shakespeare's Globe).

Television includes *Doctors* and *Rellik*.

Ammar Haj Ahmad | Said

Trained at The Higher Institute of Dramatic Arts, Damascus.

Theatre includes *The Jungle* (The Young Vic), *Love* (National Theatre and Birmingham Rep), *The Great Survey of Hastings* (Ladie's Parlour), rehearsed reading of *Goats/Told From the Inside* (Royal Court Theatre), *Kan Yama* (Cockpit Theatre), *Mawlana* (Mosaic Rooms), *The Knight and the Crescent Hare* (National Tour), *One Thousand and One Nights* (The Joey and Toby Tanenbaum Opera Centre, Toronto, and Lyceum Theatre, Edinburgh) and *Babel* (Caledonian Park).

Film includes *Maqha Almawt*, *Round Trip*, *Wada'an* and *Wall*.

Television includes *Agatha Raisin* and *Letters from Baghdad*.

Ethan Kai | Young Said / Dov

Trained at Academy of Live and Recorded Arts.

Theatre includes *Goats* (Royal Court Theatre).

Film includes *Instrument of War*.

Television includes *Doctors*, *Emmerdale* and *Mount Pleasant*.

Marlene Sidaway | Miriam

Finborough Theatre Productions include: *A Bed of Roses, Foreign Lands* and *Susan*, which subsequently transferred to the Gielgud Theatre.

Trained at East 15 Acting School.

Theatre includes *The Enchantment, A Prayer for Owen Meany* (National Theatre), *Kenny Morgan* (Arcola Theatre), *Enjoy, The Crucible* (West Yorkshire Playhouse), *Animals* (Theatre503), *Uncle Vanya* (The Print Room), *The Daughter in Law, Macbeth* (Crucible Theatre Sheffield), *Just Between Ourselves* (Royal and Derngate Theatres, Northampton), *The Lady in the Van* (Salisbury Playhouse), *A Cream Cracker Under the Settee* (Harrogate Theatre), *All My Sons* (Bristol Old Vic), *We'll Always Have Paris* (The Mill at Sonning), *Kiss Me Like You Mean It* (Soho Theatre), *A Time and a Season* (Plymouth Theatre Royal), *The Madness of Esme and Shaz* (Royal Court Theatre), *The Dearly Beloved* (Hampstead Theatre) and *Hedda Gabler* (Royal Exchange Theatre, Manchester).

Film includes *Sink, Me and Orson Welles, Venus, Oliver Twist, Tom's Midnight Garden, Beautiful Thing, I Want Candy* and *The Key*.

Television includes *Doc Martin, Doctors, Mum, Cuffs, Wallander, Hustle 8, Being Human, Survivors, The Vicar of Dibley, Kindness of Strangers, Sensitive Skin, Foyle's War, Holby City, Inspector Lynley Mysteries, Sirens* and *Life Begins*.

Radio includes *After Wonderland, Rhapsody, The Moonflask, Murder is Easy, Our Woman in Norton Tripton, The Resistance of Mrs Brown, The People Next Door* and *Siege*.

Ghassan Kanafani | Writer

Writer Ghassan Kanafani (1936–1972) is widely regarded as one of Palestine's greatest novelists, writing some of the most admired stories in modern Arabic literature. He was also an intellectual and political activist. His novellas and short stories, which have been translated into dozens of languages, are considered today to have been ahead of their time, both in form and content.

Kanafani wrote the novella *Returning to Haifa* in 1968, and published it in 1969, a testament not only to his principled commitment to the politics of liberation, but also to his deep empathy for the 'other' as well as his modern approach to storytelling. Ghassan Kanafani was assassinated by a car bomb in Beirut in 1972 at the age of 36. His young niece Lamis was with him in the car and was killed by the same bomb.

Kanafani's obituary in Lebanon's *The Daily Star* wrote that: 'He was a commando who never fired a gun, whose weapon was a ball-point pen, and his arena the newspaper pages.'

Naomi Wallace | Playwright

Finborough Theatre productions include *And I And Silence*, which subsequently transferred to Signature Theater, New York City.

Theatre includes *In the Heart of America* (Bush Theatre), *Slaughter City* (Royal Shakespeare Company), *One Flea Spare* (Public Theater, New York City), *The Trestle at Pope Lick Creek* and *Things of Dry Hours* (New York Theatre Workshop), *The Fever Chart: Three Visions of the Middle East* (Public Theater, New York City), and *Night is a Room* (Signature Theater, New York City).

Naomi has been awarded the Susan Smith Blackburn Prize twice, the Fellowship of Southern Writers Drama Award, the Obie Award and the Horton Foote Award. She is also a recipient of the MacArthur Fellowship and a National Endowment for the Arts development grant. In 2013, Naomi received the inaugural Windham Campbell Prize for Drama, and in 2015 an Arts and Letters Award in Literature. Her play *One Flea Spare* was recently incorporated into the permanent repertoire of the French National Theatre, La Comédie-Française. Only two American playwrights have been added to La Comédie's repertoire in two hundred years, the other being Tennessee Williams.

Ismail Khalidi | Playwright

Ismail Khalidi was born in Beirut and raised in the United States.

His plays include *Truth Serum Blues* and *Sabra Falling* (Pangea World Theater, Minneapolis), *Tennis in Nablus* (Alliance Theatre, Atlanta) and *Foot* (Teatro Amal, Chile). His writing has appeared in numerous anthologies as well as in *The Nation, Guernica, American Theatre, Mizna* and *Remezcla.* Ismail co-edited (with Naomi Wallace) *Inside/Outside: Six Plays from Palestine and the Diaspora.* He is currently under commission from Noor Theatre and Actors Theatre of Louisville and is a visiting artist with Teatro Amal in Chile.

Caitlin McLeod | Director

Finborough Theatre productions include *Facts, Northern Star* and *And I And Silence,* which subsequently transferred to Signature Theater, New York City.

Caitlin is the Artistic Director of new-writing company The Coterie (supported by a Sky Academy Scholarship) and has formerly been part of the Old Vic 12, Artistic Associate with HighTide and Trainee Director at the Royal Court.

Theatre includes *One Flea Spare* (Sheen Centre, New York City), *A Further Education* (Hampstead Theatre Downstairs), *BRENDA* (HighTide Festival Theatre and Yard Theatre), *Polar Bears* (West Yorkshire Playhouse), *The Malcontent* (Shakespeare's Globe), *Commonwealth* (Almeida Theatre), *HomeTruths* (Cardboard Citizens at The Bunker) and *The Children's Hour* (Royal Welsh College of Music and Drama). Caitlin has been Assistant or Associate Director for Dominic Cooke, Jeremy Herrin, James Macdonald (Royal Court Theatre), and Dominic Dromgoole (Shakespeare's Globe).

Rosie Elnile | Set and Costume Designer

Rosie was the first Resident Design Assistant at the Donmar Warehouse from 2015–2016.

Theatre includes *Goats* and *Primetime 2017* (Royal Court Theatre), *Unknown Island* and *The Convert* (Gate Theatre), *BIG GUNS* (Yard Theatre), *HARD C*CK* (Spill Festival) and *Loaded* (Jacksons Lane).

Joshua Gadsby | Lighting Designer

Trained at Royal Central School of Speech and Drama.

Theatre includes *Trap Street* and *Still Ill* (New Diorama Theatre), *The Leftovers* (The Curve, Leicester, and National tour), *A Dangerous Woman* (Birmingham Rep and National tour), *I Won't Make It On My Own* and *Consensual* (Nuffield

Theatre, Southampton), *Alligators* and *R AND D* (Hampstead Theatre),*VS* and *At the Yard* (Ponyboy Curtis at The Yard), *Rendezvous in Bratislava* and *Majesty* (Battersea Arts Centre), *Airswimming* and *Dreamplay* (The Vaults), *HARD C*CK* (Spill Festival), *RISE: Macro vs Micro* (Old Vic New Voices), *Russian Dolls* (King's Head Theatre), *The Island* (Freedom Theatre, Palestine), *I Call My Brothers* and *Caught* (Arcola Theatre), *Crave* (Prague Quadrennial), *The Sound and the Fury*, *The Devils*, *A Midsummer Night's Dream* and *Mary Stuart* (Royal Central School of Speech and Drama).

David Gregory | Sound Designer

Productions at the Finborough Theatre include *We Know Where You Live*.

Trained at the Central School of Speech and Drama and won the TTA Award for Sound in 2015 and was a nominated finalist for the OffWestEnd Award for Sound Design, also in 2015.

Theatre includes *Boudica* (Shakespeare's Globe), *Rise, Housed, 24 Hour Plays* and *Writing Festival* (Old Vic New Voices), *Red Forest* (Belarus Free Theatre, Young Vic and Italian tour), *Soap Opera* (Royal Court Theatre), *Henna Night* (Pleasance Theatre), *Bombay Roxy* (Dishoom Restaurant), *The Cunning Little Vixen* (English National Opera and Silent Opera), *Gabriel* (National tour), *Coffee and Whisky* (Ovalhouse), *Some Girl I Used To Know* (Arts Theatre and national tour),*Twelfth Night* (Watermill Theatre, Newbury, and European tour), *Our Friend the Enemy* (national tour and New York City), *The Generation of Z: Apocalypse* (Dept W), *The Grand Journey* (European tour),*The Grapes of Wrath* (Nuffield Theatre, Southampton, and national tour), *Frankenstein* (Wilton's Music Hall), *These Trees Are Made of Blood, Waiting for Godot, Lament* and *Eldorado* (Arcola Theatre), *Sleeping Beauty, The Burrowers, Alice in Wonderland, Frankenstein, Secret Adversary, Tuxedo Junction, But First This* and *Romeo and Juliet* (Watermill Theatre, Newbury), *Terrorism* (Bush Theatre), *Stalking the Bogeyman, Luce, Next Fall* and *These Trees Are Made Of Blood* (Southwark Playhouse), *Benighted* and *Dogs Of War* (Old Red Lion Theatre), *Queens of Syria* (Young Vic and national tour), *Much Ado About Nothing* (The Faction at Selfridges), *The First Man* (Jermyn Street Theatre), *When We Were Woman* (Orange Tree Theatre, Richmond), *Julius Caesar* (North Wall Theatre), *Contact.com* (Park Theatre), *Pocket Comedy, Pocket Merchant of Venice, Pocket Henry V, The Comedy of Errors, Richard III, A Midsummer Night's Dream, The Taming of the Shrew, Twelfth Night* and *The Winter's Tale* (national, European and Mexico tour for Propeller Theatre Company), *Basement Grotto* (Shoreditch Town Hall), *Five* (Saudi Arabia for National Youth Theatre), *Private Peaceful, Selfie* and *Macbeth* (Ambassadors Theatre for National Youth Theatre) and *Alexandria* (The Yard).

Lanre Malaolu | Movement Director

Larne is Co-Artistic Director of dance-theatre company *Protocol* and has formerly been part of the Old Vic 12.

Theatre includes *The Pulverised* (Arcola Theatre), *And Here I Am* (National tour and Palestine tour), *So Many Reasons* (Camden People's Theatre and Oval House) and *ADITL* (US Tour).

Film includes *Dear Mr Shakespeare*, a Sundance Film Festival selection.

Amy Whitby-Baker | Stage Manager

Finborough Theatre Productions include *The Busy World is Hushed* and *Don't Smoke in Bed*.

Theatre includes *Showcase* and *Evening of Entertainment* (The Junction, Cambridge), *Snow White* (Vienna Festival Ballet), *Peter Pan* (Motherwell Concert Hall and Theatre), *The Ends of the Earth* (Fringe Club, Hong Kong), *The Rover* (Sheffield Theatres), *Cinderella, Miracle on 34th Street* and *Dick Whittington* (Blackfriars Theatre and Arts Centre), *Jerusalem* (Sheffield University Theatre Company), *Magna Carta Festival* (Royal Holloway, University of London), *The Duchess of Malfi* and *Titus Andronicus* (University of Southampton).

Ben Karakashian | Production Manager

Finborough Theatre productions include *Home Chat*.

Trained at Royal Holloway, University of London with a BA Honours in Drama and Theatre Studies.

Theatre includes *The Grift* (Town Hall Hotel, Bethnal Green), *Grimly Handsome* (Royal Court Theatre), *Kanye the First* (HighTide Festival), *Unknown Island* (Gate Theatre), *These Trees are Made of Blood, The Plague, Richard III, Kenny Morgan, The Divided Laing* and *New Nigerians* (Arcola Theatre), *Working* and *Our Ajax* (Southwark Playhouse), *Big Guns* (Yard Theatre), *All Our Children* (Jermyn Street Theatre), *Acedian Pirates* (Theatre503), *Frontier Trilogy* (Rabenhof Theater, Vienna), *Titanic the Musical, The Mikado, Ragtime, Death Takes a Holiday* and *In the Bar of a Tokyo Hotel* (Charing Cross Theatre), *The Frontier Trilogy* (Edinburgh Festival), *The Man Who Shot Liberty Valance* (Park Theatre) and *The Bunker Trilogy* (Southwark Playhouse, Seoul Performing Arts Festival and Stratford Circus).

Lynne McConway | Producer

Finborough Theatre productions include *Vibrant 2017 – A Festival of Finborough Playwrights*.

She was a Production Assistant on *The School for Scandal* and *Skin Tight* (Park Theatre), *Gather Ye Rosebuds* (Brighton Festival) and *14/48 London* (LOST Theatre).

Production Acknowledgements

Returning to Haifa is presented by arrangement with Knight Hall Agency Ltd, Gordon Dickerson and the Kanafani Foundation.

With thanks for support to: Omar and Ghalia Al-Qattan, Ramez Sousou and Bashir Abu Manneh, as well as all those who generously donated to our crowdfunding campaign including Gary M English, Talli Somekh, Carla F Wallace, Betsy Wallace, Elizabeth Wallace and Ann Kittredge

And special thanks to: Anni and Leila Kanafani for their support of this project, and for their endless and passionate work for social justice and peace.

Press Representative | Emma Berge **emma@mobiusindustries.com**

Production rehearsed at Selladoor **www.selladoor.com**

FINBOROUGH | THEATRE

The Finborough Theatre's building – including both the Finborough Arms pub and the Finborough Theatre – celebrates its 150th birthday in 2018.

Opened in 1868, the Finborough building was designed by one of the leading architects of his day, George Godwin (1813–1888) who was also the editor of the architectural magazine *The Builder* (which is still published today), and a sometime playwright. He is buried in nearby Brompton Cemetery.

The Finborough Arms was one of five public houses originally constructed as part of the Redcliffe Estate (which replaced the farmland and market gardens that existed before), and is one of only three pubs of the original five that still survive today.

One of the Finborough Arms' most regular customers was sanitary pioneer Thomas Crapper (1836–1910) who would would regularly begin his working day in the Finborough Arms with a bottle of champagne. His daughter, Minnie, married Ernest Finch (who was born in the flat above the theatre) of the Finch family who owned and managed the building from its opening in 1868 until the early 1930s.

FINBOROUGH | THEATRE
VIBRANT **NEW WRITING** | UNIQUE **REDISCOVERIES**

'**Probably the most influential fringe theatre in the world.**'
Time Out

'**Under Neil McPherson, possibly the most unsung of all major artistic directors in Britain, the Finborough has continued to plough a fertile path of new plays and rare revivals that gives it an influence disproportionate to its tiny 50-seat size.**'
Mark Shenton, *The Stage* 2017

'**The tiny but mighty Finborough.**'   Ben Brantley, *New York Times*

Founded in 1980 on the first floor of the building (which was previously a restaurant, a Masonic Lodge, and a billiards hall), the multi-award-winning Finborough Theatre presents plays and music theatre, concentrated exclusively on vibrant new writing and unique rediscoveries from the 19th nineteenth and twentieth centuries.

Our programme is unique – we never present work that has been seen anywhere in London during the last twenty-five years.

Do visit us our website to find out more about us, or follow us on Facebook, Twitter, Instagram, Tumblr and YouTube.

For more on the history of the building and the local area, and for full information on the Finborough Theatre's work, visit our website at

www.finboroughtheatre.co.uk

The Finborough Theatre is a member of the Independent Theatre Council,
the Society of Independent Theatres, Musical Theatre Network,
The Friends of Brompton Cemetery and The Earl's Court Society;
and supports #time4change's Mental Health Charter.

Supported by

Mailing

Email admin@finboroughtheatre.co.uk
or give your details to our Box Office staff
to join our free email list.

Feedback

We welcome your comments, complaints and suggestions.
Write to Finborough Theatre, 118 Finborough Road,
London SW10 9ED or email us at admin@finboroughtheatre.co.uk

Playscripts

Many of the Finborough Theatre's plays have been published
and are on sale from our website.

On Social Media

    www.facebook.com/FinboroughTheatre

    www.twitter.com/finborough

    finboroughtheatre.tumblr.com

    www.instagram.com/finboroughtheatre

    www.youtube.com/user/finboroughtheatre

Friends

The Finborough Theatre is a registered charity.
We receive no public funding, and rely solely
on the support of our audiences. Please do consider
supporting us by becoming a member of our
Friends of the Finborough Theatre scheme.
There are four categories of Friends,
each offering a wide range of benefits.

Richard Tauber Friends

David and Melanie Alpers. J. D. Anderson. Mark Bentley.
Kate Beswick. Simon Bolland. James Carroll. Deirdre Feehan.
N. and D. Goldring. Loyd Grossman. Paul Guinery. David Harrison.
Mary Hickson. Richard Jackson. Paul and Lindsay Kennedy.
Martin and Wendy Kramer. John Lawson. Kathryn McDowall.
Ghazell Mitchell. Guislaine Vincent Morland. Carol Rayman.
Barry Serjent. Brian Smith. Lavinia Webb. Sandra Yarwood.

Lionel Monckton Friends

Philip G Hooker.

William Terriss Friends

Stuart Ffoulkes. Alan Godfrey. Ros Haigh. Melanie Johnson.
Leo and Janet Liebster.

Smoking is not permitted in the auditorium and the use of cameras and recording equipment is strictly prohibited.

In accordance with the requirements of the Royal Borough of Kensington and Chelsea:

1. The public may leave at the end of the performance by all doors and such doors must at that time be kept open.

2. All gangways, corridors, staircases and external passageways intended for exit shall be left entirely free from obstruction whether permanent or temporary.

3. Persons shall not be permitted to stand or sit in any of the gangways intercepting the seating or to sit in any of the other gangways.

The Finborough Theatre is licensed by the Royal Borough of Kensington and Chelsea to The Steam Industry, a registered charity and a company limited by guarantee. Registered in England and Wales no. 3448268. Registered Charity no. 1071304. Registered Office: 118 Finborough Road, London SW10 9ED.

The Steam Industry was founded by Phil Willmott in 1992. It comprises two strands to its work: the Finborough Theatre (under Artistic Director Neil McPherson); and The Phil Willmott Company (under Artistic Director Phil Willmott) which presents productions throughout London as well as annually at the Finborough Theatre.

Returning to Haifa

Ghassan Kanafani (1936–1972), an intellectual and
political activist, is one of Palestine's greatest novelists,
writing some of the most admired stories in modern
Arabic literature. His novellas and short stories, now
translated into dozens of languages, are widely regarded
as having been ahead of their time, both in form and
content. He was assassinated in Beirut by a Mossad car
bomb in 1972 at the age of thirty-six.

The 1969 novella *Returning to Haifa* remains one of
Ghassan Kanafani's most important and timeless works,
a testament not only to his principled commitment to the
politics of liberation, but also his deep empathy for the
'other'. This adaptation for the stage, personal, darkly
comic and ultimately hopeful, presents a deeply human
portrait of two families, one Palestinian, one Jewish,
forced by history into an intimacy they didn't choose.
And while this is a drama about the Middle East in the
1960s, it is also an undeniably timely story that speaks
to universal themes of memory, freedom and family.

Naomi Wallace's plays include *In the Heart of America* (Bush Theatre), *Slaughter City* (Royal Shakespeare Company), *One Flea Spare* (Public Theater, New York City), *The Trestle at Pope Lick Creek* and *Things of Dry Hours* (New York Theatre Workshop), *The Fever Chart: Three Vision of the Middle East* (Public Lab, New York City), *And I and Silence* (Finborough Theatre and Signature Theatre, NYC) and *Night is a Room* (Signature Theatre, NYC). Her work has received numerous awards including the Obie Award, the Horton Foote Award and a MacArthur Fellowship. In 2013, she received the inaugural Windham–Campbell Prize for Drama, and in 2015 an Arts and Letters Award in Literature. Her play *One Flea Spare* was recently incorporated in the permanent repertoire of the French National Theatre, the Comédie-Française.

Ismail Khalidi was born in Beirut and raised in the United States. His plays include *Truth Serum Blues* and *Sabra Falling* (Pangea World Theater, Minneapolis), *Tennis in Nablus* (Alliance Theatre, Atlanta) and *Foot* (Teatro Amal, Chile). His writing has appeared in numerous anthologies as well as in *The Nation*, *Guernica*, *American Theatre*, *Mizna* and *Remezcla*. He co-edited (with Naomi Wallace) *Inside/Outside: Six Plays from Palestine and the Diaspora*. He is currently under commission from Noor Theatre and Actors Theatre of Louisville, and is a visiting artist with Teatro Amal in Chile. He holds an MFA from New York University's Tisch School of the Arts.

GHASSAN KANAFANI

Returning to Haifa

the novella adapted for the stage by
ISMAIL KHALIDI *and* NAOMI WALLACE
with an introduction by Bashir Abu-Manneh

FABER & FABER

First published in 2018
The Bindery 51 Hatton Garden,
London ECIN 8HN
Typeset by Country Setting, Kingsdown, Kent CT14 8ES
Printed in England by CPI Group (UK) Ltd, Croydon CR0 4YY

A CIP record for this book is available from the British Library

978-0-571-34782-7

Ghassan Kanafani Cultural Foundation

The Ghassan Kanafani Cultural Foundation (GKCF) was founded as a Lebanese NGO on 8 July 1974, the second commemoration of the martyrdom of Ghassan Kanafani.

In addition to publishing Ghassan Kanafani's literary works, GKCF's main focus is early childhood development and education, based on the holistic approach, as well as working with young people in camps for Palestinian refugees in Lebanon.

Since 1974 GKCF has established and runs six kindergartens for young children, two habilitation centres for children with disabilities, three libraries and art centres and three clubs. More than 1,600 children benefit yearly from GKCF's projects. Around 9,500 children have so far graduated from the foundation's kindergartens.

www.ghassankanafani.org

Returning to Kanafani

Much ink has been spilt on the Israeli–Palestinian conflict. But most of it is not of the right kind. Rather than explaining or illuminating the root causes of national antagonism and contradiction, it obfuscates and obscures by invoking timeless notions of ancient hatreds and evil terror. Such language gets in the way of real historical understanding and, ultimately, reconciliation.

No one understood this basic fact better than Palestinian writer Ghassan Kanafani (1936–1972). Forced out of Acre in 1948, he roamed the Arab world in search of a secure abode. In the process, he became Palestine's most famous writer and activist intellectual: a journalist, playwright, novelist, satirist, political and historical analyst, and spokesperson for a Palestinian resistance group. His core objective was to construct a language that captured the essence of Palestinian existence as a 'complete human symbol', both of misery and challenge. Because he succeeded, Israel cut his young life short and killed him (with his niece) in a car bomb in Beirut on 8 July 1972. As his obituary in the *Daily Star* concluded: he was a 'commando who never fired a gun': 'his weapon was a ballpoint pen and his arena newspaper pages. And he hurt the enemy more than a column of commandos.'

Kanafani, then, understood that language has the potential both to corrupt and exploit and to emancipate. A *blind language* (to use a phrase he dubbed) only serves the powerful and suffocates those who seek change. To defeat it, what he needed was an effective strategy premised on self-examination and self-critique. A new language had to be imagined: critical, evaluative, and rational. If *blind language* encourages lamentation and resignation, his language would empower the circulation of democracy throughout the body politic of the Arab world. As a precursor to the Arab rebels of the present, Kanafani understood that only democracy unleashes the buried potentials of repressed and denied lives: 'What is required of us,' he said in 1968, 'is that we transform the democratic spirit into a daily practice at all levels.'

Returning to Haifa (1969), adapted here to the stage by Ismail Khalidi and Naomi Wallace, should thus be read in the context of Kanafani's struggle against a politically exploitative language. His novel is distinct in Palestinian fiction for staging a genuine political dialogue between a holocaust survivor and Palestinian refugees whose home she ends up occupying. Contra to what Kanafani calls 'a dialogue of the deaf', here stories are traded, motivations explained, suffering recounted. Clash and communication intertwine to produce one of the most memorable encounters of enemies in the annals of either Palestinian or Israeli fiction. What adds to the complexity is that Miriam Koshen, the Israeli protagonist, also adopts the Palestinian couple's infant child Khaldun, whom they were forced to leave behind during the chaotic events of their expulsion from Haifa twenty years earlier. Now in 1967, after Israel's occupation of the rest of Palestine, their child Khaldun stands in front of them as Israeli soldier Dov. What can result from their tense and tragic meeting?

Kanafani's skills as a literary realist and humanist are in full swing here. Enemies are humanised (even saved from ideologised – Zionist – versions of themselves), the injustice of dispossession is confronted head on, and a universal morality is formulated in order to protect *all* parties to the conflict. By staging a moral confrontation

8

between adversaries (rather than a violent one), Kanafani plants potential seeds of future reconciliation. The moral cause that this Palestinian articulates is one where the weak are not exploited and their mistakes are not used against them. His imagined homeland would live in the universal, and shuns the destructive particularism of nationalism and ethnic strife.

Kanafani is rigorous enough to acknowledge that such universal justice can only be achieved as a form of reciprocity and mutuality between equals. For that, struggle is required. But it is the kind of struggle that Israelis can participate in, so long as they seek to work for a humanist and just outcome in which all can share. *Returning to Haifa* is internationalist that way, and yearns for all-round transformation. If war is to be avoided, then a politics of justice has to succeed.

There is no better way to mark seventy years since the Palestinian catastrophe (the *nakba*) than to remember that Palestinians like Kanafani offered a vision of peace and justice for all. It has long been overdue for Israel to abandon its violent *blind language* and speak humanism.

BASHIR ABU-MANNEH
University of Kent

Acknowledgements

Naomi Wallace wishes to thank her mother,
Sonia De Vries, and Anni Kanafani,
for their encouragement and support

Ismail Khalidi wishes to thank
Mona, Rashid, Lamya, Dima, Caro and Nur

Returning to Haifa, presented by Lynne McConway Productions in association with Neil McPherson for the Finborough Theatre, was first presented at the Finborough Theatre, London, on 27 February 2018 with the following cast:

Safiyya Myriam Acharki
Young Safiyya Leila Ayad
Said Ammar Haj Ahmad
Young Said/Dov Ethan Kai
Miriam Marlene Sidaway

Directed by Caitlin McLeod
Set and Costume Design by Rosie Elnile
Lighting Design by Joshua Gadsby
Sound Design by David Gregory
Movement Director Lanre Malaolu
Casting Director Arthur Carrington

This adaptation was originally commissioned by New York's Public Theater, which had committed to programming the play, but subsequently abandoned the production after political pressure.

Characters

Said
a Palestinian man, mid-forties

Safiyya
a Palestinian woman, Said's wife, early forties

Miriam
an elderly Israeli Jewish woman, sixties

Dov
a young Israeli soldier and the son, twenty

Young Safiyya
Safiyya, twenty years earlier, mid-twenties

Young Said
Said, twenty years earlier, mid-twenties

*Dov should be played by the same actor
as Young Said*

Time
fluid and interconnected: 1947, 1948, 1967

Place
an imagined Ramallah and Haifa,
and the road between

Set
minimal and not realistic: always a feeling
of disjuncture, rupture, but also of worlds
unexpectedly intertwined and haunting one another

RETURNING TO HAIFA

Said and Safiyya are undressing for bed. Elsewhere, their subdued, younger selves are doing the same. Said stops unbuttoning his shirt, staring at Safiyya, shocked at having just heard her question. Then Young Said and Young Safiyya also stop undressing and are staring at her. Unless stated, Said and Safiyya neither hear nor see their younger selves, though sometimes they sense their haunting.

Said Go to. (*Beat.*) Go to – Why?

Safiyya Just to. See it.

Said To see what?

Safiyya You know.

Said Safiyya? What. What? (*Beat.*) Are you saying?

Safiyya is silent, then:

Safiyya Yes.

Said To see our.

Safiyya Yes.

Silence some moments.

Said What is this?

Safiyya Maybe to look and –

Said No. We're just tired.

Safiyya To see our house.

Said Let's get to bed. It's late . . . After so many years –

Safiyya I thought we –

Said What are you thinking?

Safiyya does not acknowledge Said's look and continues undressing.

Of him?

Hearing this question, Young Safiyya and Young Said listen, unsure. Outside, the sound of passing jeeps and of soldiers' boots striking the road can be heard. Said notices a button missing on his shirt.

I don't want to go. In the morning we'll have forgotten. There's a button missing.

Safiyya There's always a button missing with you. They've opened the borders.

Said No.

Safiyya For the first time in . . . I was just –

Said I don't want to talk about it. Damn it.

He can't close his nightshirt.

Safiyya You don't need buttons when you sleep.

Said We need to be here. To keep an eye on Khalid.

Safiyya You spoke to him? Again?

Said nods 'Yes'.

Said Told him he better buckle down on his studies. That he will not, under any circumstances, be picking up a rifle and running off to the hills. 'You're seventeen,' I said, 'and that gun you'd carry weighs half as much as you do.' He's a romantic!

Safiyya And he listened?

Young Safiyya He won't listen.

Said Of course he listened; I'm his father. Tomorrow I'll take him to the library again. I'll watch him study if I have to. More books will do the trick.

Safiyya Others are going.

Said Books will pin him down.

Safiyya Just to look.

Young Safiyya (*to Young Said*) He's thinking of going. Alone.

Said Safiyya, we aren't going. I don't care what others do.

Young Said nods as he polishes a pair of shoes with spit and his shirt sleeve. The youths are now hopeful they might go to Haifa.

Safiyya Said. Don't try to go alone.

Said looks at her, exposed and defensive, but silent for a beat.

Said Why would you say –? What? I don't want to. Ridiculous. It was your – Even the thought makes me –

He breaks off.

Safiyya Who knows how long they'll leave the border open.

Said Safiyya! Stop.

A moment of silence.

If it's a disgrace for the people of that city, for you and me it's a double disgrace. Why torture ourselves?

Young Said kneels down and, without Said registering it, puts the shoes he has just spit-shined on to Said's feet.

Safiyya But if you *are* thinking about going –

21

Said Now we certainly won't sleep.

Safiyya – take me with you.

Said I said I'm not going.

Now Said begins to say 'No' over and over again, each time as though it is a new and final 'No'. The younger selves whisper 'Yes'.

A strange morning light enters the world. The 'No's and 'Yes's build to silence, then:

We could just. Well. Maybe. Take a look?

Immediately the youths become energetic and begin to gather up clothes and finish dressing their older selves, who take over and continue on their own. When Said stalls, Young Said prods him to speed up his action. Young Said hands Said a cigarette, which he takes without acknowledging Young Said.

All right. There. We should go. Yes.

As Said and Safiyya exchange the following, Safiyya runs her hands through Said's hair, ordering it.

Safiyya Let me give you a trim.

Said You should put your hair up.

He licks his finger and wipes something from Safiyya's face. Both gestures are more pragmatic than affectionate.

Safiyya Let's say goodbye to Khalid.

Said He's studying. He's piled his books really high on his desk –

Safiyya (*calling*) Khalid!

Said Strategy – so that we can't see him.

Safiyya (*calling*) We're going out.

There is no response.

Said Leave him to his studies.

Safiyya (*calling*) There's food on the stove if you're hungry.

Said If he gets hungry enough, maybe he'll devour those books. Like I used to.

Safiyya (*to Khalid*) Don't just eat pistachios and peanuts, OK?

Said I was the same. My parents would hide the nuts from me.

Safiyya (*to Khalid*) That's not a meal. And don't leave me a pile of shells to clean off your desk.

Said (*to Khalid*) Eat whatever you want, as long as you study!

Safiyya Quiet.

Said Fine. Enough. Let's get on with it.

All four stand ready to go but none move. Said and Safiyya each turn and almost unconsciously fix something in the outfits of their younger selves, a button or a collar perhaps. The sound of an engine backfires, then starts, along with the crackle of a car radio being tuned. They pivot and enter the idea of the car journey.

Safiyya You're forehead's on fire.

Said There's no air in this car! The asphalt's burning under the wheels.

Safiyya Maybe if you quit talking and catch your breath – You've been going non-stop since we left Ramallah, about the war –

Said Which war?

Safiyya About the Mandelbaum Gate.

Said Demolished by bulldozers! Right. Of course. And how their army reached the Jordan river, then the Suez canal, then the edge of –

Safiyya – Damascus in a matter of hours.

Said Imagine. Damascus.

Safiyya And the cease-fire. You forgot to mention the cease-fire!

The following pours out of Said in a steady stream.

Said . . . And the curfews, and the soldiers plundering the houses and my cousin in Kuwait consumed with anxiety and the neighbour who gathered up his things and fled and the three Arab soldiers who fought alone for two days on the hill near Augusta Victoria Hospital, and the men who took off their army uniforms, fought in the streets of Jerusalem alone and the peasant who was killed the minute they saw him near the –

He breaks off.

Well . . . (*Beat.*) What day is it, Safiyya?

Safiyya June 30th.

Said And the year?

Safiyya You know, Said.

Said Say it.

Safiyya 1967.

Young Said *and* **Young Safiyya** 1947.

Said Yes.

A popular 1940s tune comes on the radio. Young Said and Young Safiyya begin to dance. The youths speak as they dance.

Young Said We're headed north! Across the plain, Ibn Amar –

Said Twenty years ago – It doesn't feel like. But they've renamed it. This was called the Ibn Amar plain.

Young Safiyya Ibn Amar.

Safiyya Take the Jerusalem road. None of your short cuts. For twenty years I imagined the Mandelbaum Gate would open again, that we could go back. But I never imagined –

Said – that it would be opened from the other side, huh? Never entered my mind either. Doors should always open from one side only. That they were the ones to open it, it all seems so –

Safiyya Frightening. Strange.

Said (*simultaneously*) Absurd. Comical?

Young Said There she is! There's the city!

Said Humiliating?

Young Safiyya Smell it?! I can smell the port!

Safiyya That smell . . .

Young Safiyya Like something . . . open. Opening!

Young Said A window!

Young Safiyya No, like a mouth. Like kisses!

Young Said Kisses? If you say so, my love!

Young Said tries to kiss Young Safiyya. She teasingly avoids him.

Safiyya It still smells . . . Can you smell it? Like war. Like –
This Fiat's a piece of junk.

Said It's got no pick-up on these hills. Not like the old
Ford did.

*Said changes the radio. An American/British song from
1967. The youths note the change but continue to
listen and move to it. Said changes the station again.
A man speaking Hebrew. Safiyya turns it off.*

Safiyya You don't think Khalid will leave while we're
gone?

Said Don't worry. Right now Khalid is sitting with his
nose in his algebra.

Safiyya When Khalid talks about joining the other
fighters, he's like a stranger –

Safiyya breaks off.

Said A stranger? Come on. That boy. That boy's got my
blood, *our blood*, coursing through him, bonds that may
bend, Safiyya,

Safiyya But never break. Yes, I know, I know.

Said And I know our son better than he knows himself.

Safiyya Khaled is taller than you now.

Said Barely.

Safiyya Does that bother you?

Said What?! Of course not. Let him grow as tall as a
mountain. A skyscraper! He's still my son.

Safiyya And almost a man. When he leaves for
university, it will be just us again.

Said We'll enjoy that. Lots of quiet. All kinds of quiet.

Said and Safiyya look out in silence. Young Said takes a deep, delicious breath.

Young Said Smell the markets? The thyme, the bread, the . . . Now the fish. And, there. Look, the sea!

Young Safiyya takes a deep breath.

Young Safiyya Salty water! Waves! Listen to it!

She lets out a squeal.

Young Said I'd forgotten the sea is so foreign and impressive to you village girls. Aw, my little *Fellaha*.

Young Safiyya playfully pushes him.

Safiyya I'd forgotten how the sea looks. How it really looks.

Young Safiyya It goes on and on. Keeps coming and going.

Young Said continues teasing.

Young Said Yes it *is* big, and this machine is called a 'car', Safiyya, a 'car'.

Young Safiyya Yeah. A 1946 Ford with a 59 A v-8 block engine with chrome-plated wings!

Young Said Wow.

Young Safiyya My peasant of an uncle, Azmi, works on cars for big-shot city folk like you, Said 'Basha'.

He laughs, then points ahead.

Young Said Look.

Young Safiyya We're here.

Said We're here, Safiyya.

They are all absorbed in the sights.

Safiyya I never imagined I'd see it again.

Said You're not seeing Haifa. They're showing it to you. There's a difference.

Safiyya Enough! You've been jabbering non-stop, with your philosophies and treatises on states and gates and fate and stakes.

Said Why do you think they opened the border? Just for our sakes?

Safiyya No. This is part of the war.

Said Right.

Safiyya I know that.

Said And now that they control all of it, they're saying to us, 'Help yourselves, look and see how much better we are than you, how much more developed. You should accept being servants. We've defeated you. Occupied you. Peasants that you are, admire us!'

Said takes the city in.

But look for yourself: nothing's really changed. We could have done better than they did.

Safiyya Said. Why did we come?

Young Safiyya Are you crazy, Said? Durgham?!

Young Said Then how about . . . Ziad?

Young Safiyya shakes her head 'No'.

Young Safiyya And Samir and Salim and Mahmoud are out, too, which leaves . . .

Young Said Who says it will be a boy, anyway?

Young Safiyya I told you. I knew it was a boy from the start. I can almost see him. His face.

Young Said How about . . . Muhsin?

Young Safiyya No. It's settled. We'll name our boy Khaldun.

Young Said Huh. I like the ring of that.

Safiyya Why have we come?

Young Said My son, Khaldun.

Said Just . . . Just . . .

Safiyya Sure, just to have a look.

Said recognises the old street names as they pass by. So do their younger selves. Said gets more and more excited.

Said Wadi Nisnas, Allenby Street –

Young Said Allenby was a dog.

Young Safiyya And Balfour a boar!

Said King Faisal Street –

Young Said That's a good one! Hanatir Square!

Safiyya Put both hands on the steering wheel.

Young Safiyya And Halisa?

Young Said There's something – The names. Strange. I –

Safiyya They've changed the names, Said.

Said No. I don't care. This is King Faisal Street. And over there is Hadar.

Safiyya Watch out, Said! Take it easy. Please.

Said I know where I'm going, know it like the back of my –

Safiyya You're sweating again. Looks like you've just come in from the rain.

Said How can it be so bloody hot? I wish it would rain. I brought an extra shirt so I can change if I –

Safiyya There are soldiers everywhere. Be careful.

Said There's the road down to the port. Look at the sea from here.

Safiyya This was always the best spot to see it.

Said Look.

They all look at the sea.

Young Safiyya So beautiful. That colour. Are we asleep?

Young Said I'm awake!

Safiyya Slow down!

Said I'm hardly touching the gas. I bet they tried to re-name the Mediterranean too! But there are things in this world even *they* can't change.

There is a sound like an explosion and/or a crack of gunfire.

The Safiyyas Said!

Everything comes to a stop. It is as though they've had some kind of accident. The four of them are dazed for a moment.

Safiyya You've hit something.

Said It's all right.

Safiyya What did you hit? The sidewalk?

Said Just the tyre, I think. Or a shot, maybe. It sounded like – Let me check. I'll go see.

He rises, unsteadily, and walks away from Safiyya and the 'car'. There is a huge clap of thunder, which becomes the sound of mortars. Now we are back in 1948. The youths react to the sounds and are 'separated'. Said and Safiyya feel their past encircle them, but work to remain calm as they are forced to remember.

Said For some hours it's so quiet we can hear each other breathe on the streets. The city. It's not expecting anything.

He takes off his tie as he speaks. It's morning.

Safiyya Twenty years ago.

Said April 21st.

Safiyya Hot for April. So hot even the early hours are smeared with heat.

Said speaks as he blindfolds his younger self, who is confused but motionless. Then Said spins Young Said around until he's disorientated.

Said Yes, and the British still control the city and in three weeks, on the appointed day –

Safiyya – they'll begin to withdraw. All anyone talks about is the withdrawal.

Said I'm in the centre of town when the explosions begin, and the shots. Without warning. Like thunder. An all-out attack by the Jewish forces. Thunder from the East. From Mount Carmel. Mortar shells fly across the city. And then the streets of Haifa erupt into chaos. I've got to get back home.

Noise, chaos. Young Said tries to get home, to head in the direction he believes is home. Each direction he chooses, Said blocks him with his body and shoves him back, while still giving him directions. It is a nightmarish and fierce physical struggle.

That street's closed. Try another one. No! There are armed men racing from side street to main road, main road to side street. Watch out!

Young Said Safiyya?

Said Get back home. Now! Avoid the high sections of town, near Herzl Street! Their militias've been headquartered there from the start. Turn around!

Young Said Safiyya!

Said Keep away from the business district too! Don't get between Halisa and Allenby Street, it's their strongest arms base.

Young Said This way.

Said Not that way!

Young Said I can . . . The soldiers will –

Said No! The British soldiers won't protect you. They're part of the plan. Try another street.

Young Said Where am I? . . . Where am –

Said More soldiers. Look out! Take another route. Go!

Young Said I don't know where I –

Said The streets are tangled in your head, man.

Young Said Wadi Rushmiyya . . . then the Burj . . . then Wadi Nisnas –

Said The old city, Halisa. Damn it! Watch it!

Another big explosion and both Said and Young Said stop dead. Complete stillness for a moment.

Yes. Now you remember: he's five months old today.

Said and **Young Said** (*whispering*) Khaldun.

*For some moments Young Said is frozen with fear.
Then, for the first time, he hears his older self.*

Said You taste that on your tongue? Something cold and
dark? That taste won't ever leave you.

> *Now, for a moment, Young Said looks directly at his
> older self.*

Do you sense the calamity coming your way? You should
never have left them. What errand was so important,
huh?

> *A moment of silence.*

Now hurry up. Go that way!

Young Said This way!

Said No! Not that way! Come on, come on, you know
this city like the back of your hand.

Young Said I know this city.

Said That's what you said when you went into town to
get bread, go to the bank, the papers and your shirts and
'I'll be right back, I know this city like –'

Young Said Like the back of my . . . Safiyya will worry,
she always worries.

Said Keep moving!

Young Said Closed! . . . I could . . . I should . . . Wait . . .

Said No! Go! Try again.

> *Young Said is blocked again.*

Young Said Safiyya?!

> *Young Safiyya is crouching down in their home,
> hiding, trying to disappear from the noise and chaos
> surrounding her. She seems to be holding a small shape*

*in her arms but nothing is there. She sings a quiet
lullaby to keep herself calm. When she hears her name,
she listens.*

Said Get down! Here come the bullets.

Young Said It's like they've got a thousand machine
guns –

Said They're pushing you to the coast.

Young Said – all firing at once.

Said They want you out. All of you.

Young Said No. No! I've got to get back to Halisa, back
to our home.

*Huge explosions surround them, though only the
youths react to the noise. Young Said continues to
hurl himself in different directions, only to find them
blocked by Said/British soldiers.*

The Saids Safiyya . . . !

*This time, when Young Safiyya hears her name coming
from the chaos around her, she stands. At the same
time Safiyya takes the scarf from her neck and blindfolds
Young Safiyya with it.*

Young Safiyya Said?!

Safiyya The sky's on fire.

Young Safiyya Said? Where are you?!

Safiyya Bursting with the crack of rifles. Shelling.

Safiyya The whole city is shaking.

Young Safiyya I'm waiting for you! Please.

Safiyya An ungodly orchestra of noise.

Young Safiyya Please come! Don't leave me alone.

Safiyya A racket like you've never heard.

Young Said The British are blocking our way. Why won't they help us?

Said They've left you all for dead.

Safiyya How you wish you were back in the village. Where the noise is nothing but birdsong and voices calling names down the valley . . .

Young Safiyya Hurry! I'm alone, Said!

Safiyya How you miss it. Especially now. It almost makes you cry.

Young Safiyya People are pouring into the streets leading to the port.

Young Said Women, men, children.

Safiyya The English should still be in control.

Young Safiyya Where are you, Said?

Said They're herding us towards the docks!

Safiyya A rushing wave. Panic.

Young Said They'll blast the port from the hills!

Safiyya People are tumbling one over the other –

Said – falling into rowboats waiting near the wharf.

Young Said Don't get into the boats!

Young Safiyya Help us! Said?!

Said That's right. Don't get into the boats. Get back to Halisa! To Safiyya and the baby!

>   *Young Said makes a final effort to get back through the tide of people rushing to the port.*

Young Safiyya If I stay in the house we'll be safe.

Young Safiyya and Safiyya both sing a line from the same lullaby. Safiyya speaks as her younger self continues to sing, terrified.

Safiyya Yes. Stay in the house. Don't move.

Young Safiyya But Said. He could be hurt.

Safiyya Stay where you are.

The Saids (*calling*) Safiyya!

Young Safiyya Is that his voice?

Safiyya It's not his voice.

Young Safiyya I hear his voice. He's calling!

Safiyya You're just scared. Inside here it's safe. Out there it's dangerous.

Young Safiyya looks out.

Young Safiyya I think I see him!

Safiyya No. It's a stampede. Get away from the door!

Young Safiyya That's not him. No. Where is he?

Safiyya He'll find his way back. Just wait where you are!

Young Safiyya Maybe . . . Maybe . . . I'll just . . . take a quick look outside.

Safiyya No, Safiyya!

Young Safiyya Maybe that's him, he must have lost his jacket . . . I need to see if it's him.

Safiyya No.

Young Safiyya Just a couple steps closer to see. Said?!

Safiyya Don't leave the house!

36

Young Safiyya rushes out into the chaos.

Don't! (*Quietly.*) Don't leave the child. Stupid *Fellaha*.

Young Safiyya is suddenly besieged all around by a wave of people, like a force field, pulling her from the doorway and sweeping her into the street. Said and Safiyya now step back and watch their younger selves carried away towards the sea.

Safiyya (*distant*) I'm carried away by the crowd like a twig of straw –

Said – down to the sea with heaps of others –

Safiyya – and the floating bodies between the boats.

A moment of silence.

Said How much time passes –

Safiyya – until you think of the boy? Still in his crib in Halisa.

Young Safiyya makes a heroic effort to get back to her home but it's too late.

Young Safiyya Khaldun! . . . Khaldun!

Finally Young Said reaches Young Safiyya. She turns away from him to get back, but they are both carried along by the unstoppable crowd. The sound of the chaos becomes the sea, engulfing them. The youths become still.
Slowly, as though underwater, they remove their blindfolds and look at one another. Then they disappear. Swallowed. Said and Safiyya are left alone in silence for some moments.

Said This is the road.

They continue the journey.

Safiyya Yes. Slow down a bit. I can hear your heart; it's that loud.

Said (*attempts a laugh*) Like a blow from a rock, over and over.

Safiyya Look. There's the building the priest's family owned.

Said Halul Street.

Safiyya That's where the Arab fighters barricaded themselves in.

Said Fought to the last bullet, the last man.

There is a strange noise, like a seam tearing apart, when they first see their house.

Safiyya There. There it is.

Said I'll park here, in my old spot, like I always did when –

He cuts himself off abruptly. They leave the idea of the car and look up at the idea of their house.

Safiyya Still with its coat of yellow paint.

Said The green iron gate.

Safiyya There's a new clothes-line fixed to the pegs on the balcony. My pegs . . .

Said Pencil marks on the wall.

Safiyya My balcony . . . The fourth step still broken in its centre. I broke it, remember? I dropped a –

Said I broke that step, I dropped the . . . Ah, the grille work of the *masatib*.

Safiyya Mahjub es-Sa'adi's place.

Said So quiet.

38

Safiyya Two, three. These last steps to the second floor. My feet remember. Five, six, seven.

Said The door.

Safiyya Eight . . . nine . . .

They stand looking at the imaginary door.

It's been repainted. What *is* that colour?

Said They changed the bell. (*Beat.*) And the name, naturally.

Said forces a smile and takes Safiyya's hand.
He 'rings' the bell. We hear slow footsteps that seem to come from far away, then suddenly close. Then the muffled sound of a bolt creaking and a door opening slowly. They see Miriam before we do.

So this is she.

He seems frozen. Safiyya steps forward.

Safiyya Hello. May we come in?

Suddenly Miriam, an elderly woman, appears from elsewhere. But they continue to speak as though she's in front of them. Miriam stares elsewhere too, as though she's seeing them in front of her. Some moments in silence. A feeling of disjuncture.

Miriam I've been expecting you for a long time.

With a 'thump' the light cuts to black for a beat and then back on, revealing Said and Safiyya standing in front of Miriam but now on opposite sides. They face each other.

Said Do you know who we are?

Miriam nods several times. No one moves. Miriam steps aside as they enter the 'house' so that she speaks to their backs.

Miriam You are the owners of this home. I know that.

Said and Safiyya turn.

Said *and* **Safiyya** How do you know?

Miriam smiles at them.

Miriam From everything.

She looks around, slightly confused herself.

From the photographs that were. Left behind. From the way the two of you stood. At the door. From –

Said speaks to no one in particular.

Said The rug on the wall. From Syria. My great-uncle, he – You kept it.

Safiyya Your picture of Jerusalem.

Said Of course you kept it.

Safiyya The pottery from the Armenian's place, in the old city . . .

Said It's beautiful, no?

Miriam Yes. The colours.

Said glances around the room.

Said But not my books. All my books. Who –

Miriam Men came. Took them away.

Said Ah, yes.

Miriam They said it was state business. It happened when we first moved in. There was a lot of . . . coming and going.

Said Coming and going. Of course.

Safiyya But she kept so much. Why not the books?

Miriam Officials came to get them. The books. Went to a library.

Said Hugo and Balzac, in French? They *went*? The Naguib Mahfouz I bought in Cairo the year before, *went*? My Tennessee Williams? My notes in the margins . . .

Miriam We had no time to read.

Said Someone is reading my notes. Somewhere.

Safiyya Arabic notes in a French novel.

Said French notes in the Arabic books.

Miriam But certainly you've replaced them by now?

Said Those colossal Oxford dictionaries.

Safiyya I could barely lift them.

Said And Melville. A whale, a whale. A good story for us all.

Miriam changes the subject:

Miriam Every day these past three weeks, many Arabs . . . Many people have come around here –

Said 'Cherries! Cherries! Cherries!'

Miriam – have come looking at houses and going into them.

Said 'Oh, Flask, for one red cherry ere we die!'

Miriam And every day I thought surely they will come.

There is a moment of silence.

Said And now we have come.

Miriam Yes.

They each glance around, tracing over the objects in the 'house'.

What happened . . . I'm sorry. I never thought things would be the way they are. Now.

Safiyya avoids eye-contact with Miriam and speaks through Said. Said and Miriam speak English together. Safiyya speaks some English but mostly she speaks through Said in Arabic. Miriam does not speak Arabic.

Safiyya Where is she from?

Said She wants to know where you are –

Miriam Poland. I came from Poland.

Said When?

Miriam 1948.

Said When exactly? The date.

Miriam March. The first of March.

An awkward silence between them.

Said We didn't come to tell you to get out of here.

Miriam nods.

. . . That would take a war, after all. I mean to say, your presence . . . Here. In this house, our house, it's another matter. We only came to look. At our things. Maybe you can understand that.

Miriam I do. I understand.

Said Good. We won't need much time. Just to look.

Miriam I understand. But –

Said cuts her off, but calmly.

Said But? This terrible, enduring 'but' . . . Yes, but? . . . *But what? But* it is our house now, *but* you fled, *but* finder's keepers, *but* tough luck, *but* know your place, *but* don't get any ideas, *but* you don't exist. You don't ex—

He cuts himself off. He paces several times back and forth but then suddenly notices something and stops. He points at it.

Said The feathers!

Miriam What?

Said Peacock feathers! There were seven of them in that vase.

Safiyya My sister gave me that vase.

Said Seven. There are only five there. Two feathers are missing.

Miriam Are they? I didn't –

Said What happened to them? Did men in uniforms confiscate them also?

Miriam is baffled by the question.

Miriam I don't know where the two feathers you speak of went. I can't remember.

Now Miriam speaks while Said and Safiyya listen, sometimes moving away to look at things in the room, sometimes touching invisible objects they remember. Most of the lines from Said and Safiyya during Miriam's story are between themselves.

Miriam I'd like to tell you how we –

Said You don't need to.

Miriam *Thieves in the Night*. Arthur Koestler. You know it? My husband, Iphrat, read the book to me while we were waiting in Milan.

There is a moment when Said looks at Miriam, deciding. Then he translates for Safiyya.

Said *Thieves in the Night* by someone called Koestler?

43

*This means nothing to Said and Safiyya. Miriam
wonders what they are saying.*

Miriam I'm sorry. I don't understand Arabic.

Said Of course. Of course. My wife Safiyya understands
some English, but still I must translate.

Miriam What I mean is that for us, Isra— Palestine was
nothing more than a stage set adapted from an old
legend –

Said A stage set. Palestine.

Miriam – still decorated in the manner of Christian
books for children in Europe.

Said Holy Land.

Safiyya Angels and virgins?

Said And donkeys.

Miriam Of course we didn't fully believe the land was
only a desert rediscovered by the Jewish Agency after two
thousand years –

Safiyya Shepherds guarding their flocks on the hillside?

Said Shepherds that looked like us.

Miriam But that wasn't what mattered most to us then –

Said Like the old prints they sell to foreigners in
Jerusalem –

Miriam interrupts them, firmly.

Miriam We didn't choose Haifa. (*Beat.*) We'd been
placed in a residence choked with others where something
called 'waiting' made up our daily concerns. We reached
Haifa via Milan, from Warsaw. In March. Of '48. Until
then we had no idea we'd end up here, nor had Iphrat or
I ever met an Arab in our entire life. In fact, it was in

44

Haifa, a year and a half after the war . . . that we came upon our first Arab.

Said looks eye to eye with the eye of the peacock feather.

Said A real Arab? And in the wild?

Miriam Well. Maybe I should . . . Let me get you something to drink. Something to eat? What can I offer you?

Said Tea.

Safiyya (*to Said but looking at Miriam*) I'm hungry. Ask her to make me some *mahshee*. Or some *maqloobee*. Maybe we can celebrate with *mansaf*? Or does she do *shushbarak*? That would be a treat. Have you not cooked us something for our return?

Miriam, not understanding, nods anyway and disappears. We hear her slow steps echoing down the hall.

Said Safiyya, are you –

Safiyya closes her eyes, mapping the house.

Safiyya Shh. She's going down the hall . . . leading to the kitchen. On the right, the bedroom. Our bedroom. On the wall the drawing my mother made of my face . . . Perhaps she got rid of it. Yes, I'm sure she did. On the left a mirror, then a smaller room –

They hear a door slam.

As if she's in her own house. She acts as if it's hers!

They smile at one another.

The mint tea I made, from the bush in the garden, remember? So many leaves. And the sugar. I was never shy with sugar. Her tea will taste nothing like –

45

Miriam returns. Her footsteps seem to continue even when she has stopped walking. Miriam takes up where she left off.

Miriam Water. It has to boil.

Said You were saying?

Miriam Yes. There was fighting. During those months.

Said Yes. There was fighting.

Safiyya We remember.

Said Go on.

Miriam But we kept in our minds that mythical picture, in perfect harmony with what we had imagined all our lives. What we'd been told.

Said You, the angels, and us, the shepherds.

Safiyya Let her finish.

Miriam The fighting we heard and read about every morning in the papers seemed to be taking place between men and ghosts, nothing more. (*Beat.*) In '48 we were at the Emigrés' Lodge. At least, that's what we called it. We stayed there for several days after that decisive battle in April –

Said Battle?

Miriam We could tell it was over.

Said To call it a battle is . . .?

Miriam That with the help of the British –

Said Yes, with the *help* of the British.

Miriam – they had taken the city so quickly.

Said They?

Miriam The Jewish soldiers.

Said Quickly. That's right. The British leaked the early departure date to you . . . them. Delivered Haifa straight into their hands. From hill to port. Just like that.

Miriam Yes. And when Iphrat and I finally went out, we were immediately struck by the fact that we didn't see any cars. It was a true Sabbath! It brought tears to our eyes. Iphrat's tears were tears of joy. But mine . . . I said to him, 'I am crying for another reason. Yes, this is a true Sabbath. But there is no longer a Sabbath on Friday, nor one on Sunday.' Do you understand what I am saying?

With this question, Said and Safiyya now become fully focused on Miriam.

That was just the beginning. For the first time since our arrival, I began to call Iphrat's attention to something troubling which we had neither counted on nor thought about. The signs of destruction that took on another meaning. But Iphrat refused to let himself worry or even think about it.

Said To think about what?

Safiyya To think about . . . ?

Miriam You see, I lost my father. At Auschwitz. Eight years before. They raided the house where Iphrat and I lived at the time. He wasn't home, so I hid with the upstairs neighbours. The German soldiers didn't find anyone but on their way back down the stairs they came upon my ten-year-old brother. He must have been on his way to tell me that our father had been sent to the camps. When he saw the German soldiers, he turned and ran. My brother could run very fast. In a race, he was faster than me! And I was – I saw it all through a narrow slit between the stairs. They shot him.

Miriam is somewhere else for a moment.

For me the situation here changed the day we passed near Bethlehem Church in Hadar. I saw two young men from the Haganah carrying something, which they put in a small truck near by. In a flash I saw what they were carrying. I grabbed Iphrat's arm. 'Look!' I said. But he didn't see anything. The two men were wiping their palms on the sides of their khaki uniforms. But I saw it.

Safiyya What?

Said What did you see?

Miriam It was covered with blood. Iphrat guided me across the street and asked me, 'How do you know it was an Arab child?'

Safiyya A child?

Miriam 'Didn't you see how they threw it on to the truck, like a piece of wood?' I said. If it had been a Jewish child they would never have done that. (*Beat.*) By the time we got back to the Emigrés' Lodge, I'd decided to leave.

    Said takes Safiyya's arm.

Said Let's go, Safiyya. There's no reason to stay any longer.

Safiyya No. I want to stay . . . What did she –?

Said Let's go. Thank you, madame.

Miriam Wait. Please. I'm not finished.

Said I'm sorry, but we can't –

Miriam (*firmly, certain*) I must finish. (*Beat.*) A week later, as I was making arrangements to return to Italy, Iphrat came back from a trip to the Jewish Agency with two bits of news. Good news: we had been given a house in Haifa.

Said Our house.

Safiyya To live in. We know.

Miriam Yes. But . . .

Said What was the other bit of . . . good news?

For a moment Miriam is unsure how to answer.

Miriam The two feathers you say are missing?

Said There were seven of them. Exactly.

Miriam I remember now: Dov played with them when he was little. He must have lost them.

Said *and* **Safiyya** Dov?

Miriam Dov. Yes.

Said Your son?

Miriam Yes.

Safiyya (*to Said*) What is she –

Miriam He was the second piece of news.

Safiyya What? What news? I'm –

Miriam And the reason I stayed. Why I am here in this house.

Said Dov.

Miriam I don't know what his name used to be. Or if it matters.

Said His name?

Safiyya (*quietly*) Khaldun.

Again there is the sound of something tearing open.

Miriam Tura Zonshtein, the divorced woman who had just moved in next door, she heard a baby crying and broke open the door. She couldn't care for the child so she brought it to the Jewish Agency. It was Iphrat's luck to come into that office a few minutes later. When the officials saw from his papers that he didn't have any children, they offered him a house right here in Haifa, in Halisa, as a special concession. If he agreed to adopt the child. The whole situation seemed to my husband to be a gift from God.

Said A gift from God . . .

Miriam Yes. From God. That's what he . . . Iphrat thought a child would change me completely.

Safiyya (*echoing her*) Change me.

Miriam Completely. Yes. And put a stop to the strange ideas that had been filling my mind ever since. Since I'd seen the dead Arab child . . .

Said And he was right.

Miriam He was right. And on the 29th of April –

Said (*to Safiyya*) The 29th.

Miriam 1948, yes. Accompanied by two men from the Jewish Agency, a short one and a tall one, and carrying a five-month-old boy, we entered your house. This house. The 29th, I'm sure of that.

Said I tried to get back. That day. The 29th. And other days. But the 29th, I — It was a Thursday . . .

Miriam The things that were here – Your things that were here, we –

Said But there was no way in.

Miriam Well, you had good taste.

Said Every road leading to a dead end –

Miriam And we had nothing. Not a chair to sit on. Not a lamp, a rug –

Said – a fence, a checkpoint, a bayonet forcing me to turn back.

Miriam And after a while –

Safiyya We couldn't speak to each other when you returned to the camp.

Miriam – those things felt like our things. Like home.

Said Numb. An abyss. We moved as if inside it.

Safiyya We didn't sleep for –

Said Will he? When . . . ?

Safiyya . . . Years, it seems.

Said When . . . When will he –?

Safiyya Get here?

Miriam It's time for him to be back now. He's late.

Said turns away. Safiyya keeps her eyes on Miriam.

Dov's never home on time. He's just like his father. He was always . . .

She turns away for a moment. Said feels as though he's been hit by an electric shock.

He looks a lot like you. Dov. I'd like you to wait for him. So you can talk to each other and this matter will end. As it naturally should.

Said End? Naturally?

Miriam Please. Do you think this hasn't been as much of a problem for me as it's been for you?

Said just stares at Miriam as an answer.

Safiyya I don't understand what she's saying, Said.

Said Yes, you do.

Safiyya No. Not a word of this makes sense.

Miriam For the past twenty years I've been confused, but now is the time for us to finish the matter. I know who his father is. And I also know that he is my son.

Safiyya And I know who his mother is.

Miriam He's an adult now. Let's call on him to decide.

Said To decide?

Miriam He's old enough and we must recognise that he's the only one who has the right to choose. Do you agree?

Said moves around the room. He counts the feathers again. Miriam watches him.

I'll leave you alone to discuss it.

She leaves. Again the footsteps are strange, now like many. Said looks at Safiyya questioningly.

Safiyya Khaldun.

Said Yes.

Safiyya He will be / here –

Said He will choose.

Safiyya Choose? Said, he . . . We are his real parents.

Said Yes. Of course. They stole him.

Safiyya All those times we tried to find him. When we tell him how we searched and searched for him –

Said But they've taught him how to be, day by day, hour by hour with his food, his drink, his sleep, his –

Safiyya Said. He's our Khaldun. He will choose to be with us.

She laughs nervously.

I can't believe it. No, I believe it. Yes. I've always believed it.

Said But Khaldun, or Dov, he might not know us from Adam. (*Beat.*) Maybe we should – we should get the hell out of here, Safiyya.

Safiyya What? No.

Said But what if he never knew? Or maybe he learned it a month ago, a week ago, a year?

Safiyya What does it matter? We'll take him home. And he'll understand everything.

Said But what if he was deceived? And perhaps became even more enthusiastic in the deception than they were? The crime began twenty years ago. The day we left him here.

Safiyya But we didn't leave him! You know that –

Said Yes, sure. We shouldn't have left anything. Not Khaldun, not the house, not Haifa!

Safiyya It wasn't our fault. The soldiers were blocking all the roads –

Said For years, the meetings with the Red Cross and –

Safiyya I was sure I heard you calling me outside. Just a few / steps –

Said – the waiting in line for hours, for days, with all the others, trying to get back.

Safiyya What else could we do? We had no –

Said Didn't the same feeling come over you that came over me as we drove through Haifa? As though you knew the city but it refused to acknowledge you? Haifa ignored me, Safiyya. It ignored us.

Safiyya It's the same feeling here. In this house.

Said Exactly. And what if the same thing happens with Khaldun?

Safiyya It won't, Said. How many times have you said we carry our children inside us? That our children are our –

Said Breath. Yes, our breath. My breath. But I can hardly breathe.

Safiyya We told ourselves a lie, that we'd given up hope of ever finding Khaldun. That lie made our lives endurable.

Said Yes. And there's a hole inside me, a hole I've tried to make smaller every day for twenty years . . .

Safiyya And that's where Khaldun has been waiting for us. We must trust. We must have faith in . . . it. Him. This.

Said is silent for a beat.

Said How could the boy not feel us all these years?

Safiyya Impossible. Let me fix your shirt.

Safiyya tidies Said's shirt.

We want you to look – Oh.

Said What is it?

Safiyya A button is missing.

Said What did I tell you? There's always a button missing.

Safiyya Because you always pull at your shirt like it's choking you.

Said Where do they go, these missing buttons? Imagine if they all went to the same place, thousands of them, and all of them missing, all of them –

54

Suddenly Said jumps up; he is consumed by a ferocious energy.

Do you know what happened to Faris al-Lubda?

Safiyya Our neighbour in Ramallah?

Said Just the other day, he hired a car to take him from Jerusalem to the coast, to Jaffa. Went straight to his house there, in the Ajami quarter, behind the Greek Orthodox school. That's where Faris lived twenty years ago with his family.

Safiyya Faris went in?

Said By the time he got there he was boiling with anger. He bound up the stairs two at a time and he banged on the door of his house.

It felt like an eternity as he listened to the footsteps approaching from the other side. Finally, the door opened. A hand reached out to greet him but Faris ignored it and spoke words he had held inside for all these years, that he'd rehearsed again and again in his dreams: 'I've come to look at my house,' he said. 'It's mine. And your presence here is a sorry comedy that will end some day by the power of the sword. If you wish to shoot me right now then go ahead, but know that this is still my house.'

Said breaks off.

Safiyya And?

Said The man bursts out laughing. Then he embraces Faris: 'Settle down, man!' he says. 'Save it. I'm an Arab, from Jaffa, a Palestinian, just like you. I know who you are. You're Faris al-Lubda. Come in, I'll make coffee'. So Faris enters. And he can hardly believe it.

Safiyya The house was as he'd left it?

55

Said Exactly as he'd left it! Even the smell.

Safiyya And what did he do?

Said Faris was frozen. Staring at the wall.

Safiyya Why? What was it?

Said A picture. The picture which hung on the wall rooted him into the stone beneath his feet.

He whispers, 'Badr.'

Safiyya Who?

Said The portrait of his brother, Badr. It was still the only picture on the walls. Faris hadn't seen it since he had left. You see, Badr had been the first to take up arms in '47; the first to resist what was being done in Jaffa.

Safiyya Badr was killed. He was killed, wasn't he?

Said nods 'Yes'.

Said Yes. Carried home on the shoulders of his comrades in '48. His rifle, like his body, was smashed in two by a grenade on the road to Tel-al-Rish. All of Ajami escorted Badr al-Lubda's body through the streets to his family's house. His mother had taken down everything else so that only his picture stood on the wall. And now, twenty years later, Faris could see the same nail heads which had held up the other pictures, still protruding from the empty walls. Like men standing at attention in front of Badr. When Faris and his family had fled by boat to Gaza, they left everything behind.

Safiyya Even the picture?

Said Yes. And the man who moved in, a shell had destroyed his house in the Manshiyya district during the fighting, and when he returned to the abandoned city with some of the other fighters, they arrested him. He was held in a prison camp for God knows how long.

When he was released, he refused to leave Jaffa. He saw the house and managed to rent it.

Safiyya From whom?

Said The government.

Safiyya Their government.

Said Yes, they're the landlords now.

Safiyya And the picture, it was –

Said – the first thing the man had seen. Maybe it's why he rented the house. Jaffa was a ghost town when he got out. An occupied city. Not a single Arab could be seen. He was alone in a sea of hostility. 'You didn't experience that agony,' the man told Faris. 'I did. And I found consolation in that picture. A friend in all this silence, to remind me we were here before, that it wasn't a dream like they want us to believe. To have as a companion, someone who bears arms for his freedom and yours is precious, especially for those of us who remained. Your brother became part of our family. For twenty years. And he helped us to resist. We resist by staying,' he said. (*Beat.*) Faris sat and stared at his brother Badr's image. And when he finally got up, he asked if he could take the picture with him. 'He is your brother,' the man answered, 'above and beyond anything.' So Faris al-Lubda took the picture and left behind a void, a meaningless rectangle on the wall. He then set off for Ramallah. And the whole way, he keeps looking at Badr, there on the seat beside him. But suddenly a feeling comes over Faris.

Safiyya What? What feeling?

Said Well, he can't explain why but he orders the driver to turn around and return to the coast.

When they arrive back at the house in Jaffa just after dawn, the man is there, waiting for him. He hasn't slept.

And he says to Faris: 'After you left I realised . . . If you want the picture back you must also reclaim Jaffa. The house. Us. The picture doesn't solve your problem, Faris, but it's a bridge, your bridge to us, and ours to you. Do you understand?' Faris returned to Ramallah. Without his brother's picture. Left it in Jaffa. He understood, see. (*Beat.*) Faris carries arms now, Safiyya. He is with the Fedayeen. He chose. Or it chose him, maybe, but . . .

A motor rumbles to a stop nearby. Miriam appears.

Miriam He's here.

The tired footsteps of a young man are heard climbing stairs. The closer they get the more they seem to echo, to come from several directions, perhaps even from more than one person. In this moment we hear what Safiyya and Said are thinking:

Safiyya He'll be taller than his father.

Said A handshake or a hug? No, not a hug.

Safiyya He was a long baby.

Said I bet his feet are big like mine.

Safiyya The second toes were crooked, like Said's.

Said Hopefully not the ears of Safiyya's father.

Safiyya A birthmark on his collar bone.

Said Bet he's good at math.

Safiyya What if he has a laugh like Said's mother? Oh God.

Said I hope he isn't moody. Safiyya says I'm moody –

Safiyya What if he's got too much to pack? The Fiat's small. Smaller than the Ford.

Said His hands will be large as plates, just like his brother Khalid's.

Safiyya We could ask her to mail him his things. Whatever he leaves behind.

Said Safiyya will cry when she sees him.

Safiyya I'm going to giggle, I know it.

Said No air in this room.

Safiyya Like I used to when my father scolded us.

Said If the three of us get straight in the car and drive home, Khalid will still be awake when we arrive.

Safiyya He's here.

Said Here he is.

Safiyya It's him.

Then a silence before the sound of keys fumbling and a door opening.

Dov (*offstage*) Mamma?

Another strange noise, something tearing, followed by a silence.

Miriam He's wondering why I'm in the living room at this hour.

More hesitant footsteps.

(*Calls.*) Come here, Dov. There are some guests who wish to meet you.

Suddenly Dov appears, but from a different direction than Said and Safiyya are looking. He wears an olive green military uniform, unmistakably Israeli military greens. But he strongly resembles Young Said. He is at first confused. Silence some moments. Said seems to collapse internally, in the face of Dov.

Said Is this your surprise? Is this what you wanted us to wait for?

He turns from Dov but Safiyya takes Dov in, almost in a trance.

Miriam Dov. I would like to present your parents. Your original parents.

Dov takes off his cap. He's not sure what to do with it. For some moments he loses his composure and is subdued. He makes eye-contact with Safiyya. He speaks gently. It is genuine but also slightly soldierly.

Dov I don't know any mother but you. As for my father, he was killed in the Sinai eleven years ago.

Said (*to himself*) My God, after all this it's like a cheap melodrama.

Dov What did they come for?

Miriam Ask them.

Dov stiffly obeys, as though following an order.

(*To Said, politely.*) What do you want, sir?

Said Nothing.

Dov Nothing?

Said Nothing . . . We're just –

He breaks off. Lost, incredulous. Silence some moments.

Dov It's impossible.

Said Yes. Impossible.

Dov Really. It's incredible.

Said You're in the army?

Dov looks down at his uniform and back at Said.

Dov (*wryly*) No. I'm a street-cleaner.

Said And who are you fighting for?

Dov shakes his head in exasperation.

Said Who are you fighting?

Dov You've no right to ask me these questions.

Said How come?

Dov Because you're on the other side.

Said *I'm* on the other side?

He laughs, as though trying to push out all the anguish in his chest. Then silence.

Dov I see no reason to laugh.

Said I thought it might help.

Dov Help how?

Said What?

Dov How might it help?

Said What are you talking about?

Dov You see? It's impossible.

Said You said that before. You're repeating yourself.

Dov shrugs. Said lights a cigarette. The two men now pace nervously, almost reflections of each other. Suddenly Dov stops.

Dov I think we need to talk. Like civilised people. Okay?

Said Ah. A negotiation?

He holds out a cigarette for Dov and Dov accepts.

Safiyya What does he mean by 'civilised'?

Said Nothing. Nothing.

Dov nervously tries to light his cigarette but cannot.
Said offers his and Dov lights his cigarette from Said's.
For a moment their faces almost touch but then they
both pull back.

Said I thought we were on opposite sides. What happened, huh? Now we are negotiating?

Dov Listen, I had no . . . no idea Miriam and Iphrat weren't my real parents till three or four years ago. I am. From the time I was small I was. I am a Jew.

Said A what?

Dov A Jew.

Said Really?

Dov Yes. An Israeli. I speak Hebrew, not Arabic. I –

Said And you wear your uniform and go to temple?

Dov And I eat kosher, too, yeah. Like everyone. Look, when she told me I wasn't their child it didn't change a thing. And even when she told me, later on, that my original parents were Arabs, it –

Said Arabs?!

Dov Didn't change a thing.

Said Palestinians.

Dov Nothing changed. After all, in the end, man is a cause, right, and –

Said What did you say?

Dov What?

Said 'Man is a cause'? Who said that?

Dov I don't know. I. I don't remember. Why?

Said Curiosity.

Dov Curiosity?

Said Yes. Because that's what's been going through my mind. At this very moment.

Dov That man is a cause?

Said Yes. Exactly.

They look one another over.

Dov What did you expect?

Said We expected nothing –

Dov Then why did you come looking for me?

Safiyya (*to Said*) Tell him we only came to –

Said – to look at the house.

Dov And not at me?

Said We didn't even know if you were . . . But here you are. And so are we.

Dov tries to pick up where he left off, and seems to be trying to remember something once learned by heart and unsure how to finish. He begins again abruptly:

Dov After I learned that you were . . .

Said Arabs.

Dov That you were Arabs –

Said Palestinians?

Dov Whatever you like!

Said Shepherds?

Dov Please, I . . . You see, once I learned the truth –

Said The truth.

Dov Yes. Once I learned the truth I kept asking myself:

how could a father and mother leave their five-month-old son behind and run off? And how could a mother and father not his own raise him, love him and educate him. It's been twenty years –

Said Really? Twenty years? Is that how long it's –

Safiyya Let him finish.

Dov I haven't been in direct combat yet. So perhaps in the future I'll be able to confirm to you what I'm about to say now: I belong here. And this woman is my mother. I don't know the two of you. And I don't feel anything – I don't feel anything special towards you.

Said stares at Dov for a beat before speaking. There is a new coldness in his voice.

Said There's no need for you to describe your feelings to me . . . Perhaps your first battle will be with a Fida'i, a fighter. Perhaps his name will be Khalid. Khalid is my son. Notice I didn't say he's your brother. As you said, man is a cause. Last week Khalid joined the Fidayeen.

Safiyya Why are you saying that? Khalid didn't –

Said Wait. (*To Dov.*) Do you know why we named him Khalid and not Khaldun? Because we always thought one day we'd find you.

Dov And now you've found me.

After a moment:

Said No. We didn't find you. Not yet. And I don't believe we ever will.

Safiyya What are you saying, Said?

Said (*to Safiyya*) He asks how a father and mother could leave their infant child and run off. (*To Miriam.*) Madame, you did not tell him the truth. And when you

64

did tell him, it was too late. Are we the ones who are responsible for him being left? Are we the ones who killed that child near Bethlehem church in Hadar? The child whose body was the first thing that shocked you here? Things done in your name, madame. Maybe that child was Khaldun? Maybe the small thing that died that wretched day was actually our Khaldun?

Dov begins to withdraw into himself.

Safiyya (*to Said*) Tell him how we went to the Red Cross, the UN, how we begged our foreign friends for help, how we petitioned –

Said (*to Miriam*) Maybe this young man is just an orphan child you found in Poland or England or Italy.

Now Safiyya directs her words to Dov, even if he can't understand her.

Safiyya How the boats took us away. How we ended up in Lebanon then Syria, then through Jordan and across the river and up to Ramallah. But we couldn't get back. Said. Tell him how we searched –

Said nears Dov.

Said Man, in the final analysis, is a cause.

Safiyya – for years and years and –

Said That's what you said.

Dov What is she –

Said And it's true. But what cause? That's the question.

Safiyya now stares off somewhere else, as the men talk.

Dov That is the question?

Said Exactly. So think carefully. Khalid is also a cause, not because he's my son. When we take a stand as a human being, it has nothing to do with flesh and blood and identity cards and passports. . . . Can you understand that?

Dov I'm listening.

Said Good.

Suddenly Said notices a piece of tobacco on Dov's lip. Almost automatically he moves to remove it. Dov freezes. Only when Said has removed the tobacco does he realise that he's touched Dov and it effects them both.

A bit of tobacco. There on your lip.

Dov Oh. Go on. Go on.

Said So let's imagine that you received us – as we've dreamed for twenty years – with kisses and tears and embraces. Would that have changed anything? Even if you had accepted us, would we accept you? Let your name be Khaldun, Isma'il or anything else –

Dov My name is Dov.

They regard one another fiercely. Said repeats his name steadily:

Said Dov? Dov. Dov. Dov –

Dov Stop. Stop saying my name.

Said All right. But in spite of it all, I don't feel any scorn towards you. The guilt isn't yours alone.

Dov I don't feel any guilt.

Said No? Then maybe guilt will become your fate from now on. Besides that, what else is there? You know, I dreamed –

He stops abruptly.

Dov You dreamed? So now you're going to get sentimental.

Said laughs. Strangely, Dov laughs too.

Said So we agree that a human being is made up of nothing more than what's injected into him day after day over a lifetime?

Dov Sure.

Said If I regret anything, it's that I believed the opposite. For so many years. I believed –

Dov What did you dream then? Of me?

Said Not of you, no. Of Khaldun. (*Beat.*) Did you feel it?

Dov You've got to be fucking kidding me –

Said (*abruptly*) Somewhere inside you, in a place that may not even exist, did you feel us, longing for you, dreaming of you –

Dov is disturbed by this question but masks it.

Dov How could I? I'm Dov. Not –

Said Yes. Of course. You are Dov.

Said paces again, then suddenly stops. He speaks to Safiyya.

What is home, Safiyya? Or a homeland?

Safiyya Why are you asking me this?

Said Is it these chairs that remained in this room? The table? Some feathers?

Safiyya's and Said's eyes meet and for a moment they look at each other in silence.

Or is it the picture of Jerusalem on the wall? The copper lock? Some old, gnarled tree? Is it Khaldun? Our illusions about him? Is it the picture of a dead brother?

Safiyya Said, stop.

Said Or is it the sight of you, on the balcony, leaning over, watching for me to come home, your long black braid swinging? You were radiant then –

He stares hard at Safiyya until she feels self-conscious.

Safiyya What are you saying? That I wasted my youth, waiting for this moment? Never knowing how terrible it would be?

Said looks Safiyya in the eye, perhaps for the first time in a long while.

Said I'm saying: I can find no resemblance between him and our son Khalid.

Safiyya That if I had not loved you so much and stayed in that house with our son, not run out into the streets like a stupid girl then this would be . . .? I lost both of you. I was young and I . . .

Said Safiyya. We've both lived without our son.

As they are speaking, Dov now moves to stand stiffly in front of them, challenging them.

Dov Perhaps none of this would have happened if you hadn't run? If you hadn't been such cowards but had stayed and fought?

Said Cowards?

Dov None of you should have left Haifa. If that wasn't possible, then no matter what it took, you shouldn't have left an infant in its crib.

And if that was also impossible, then you should never have stopped trying to return. You say that too was impossible?

Suddenly, involuntarily it seems, Dov grabs hold of Said's face and looks into him.

Twenty years have passed, man. Twenty years!

Miriam Dov, please! They're our –

Dov What did you do all that time, huh?

Miriam – guests.

Dov What did you do to reclaim your son? All those years. If I were you I would've taken up arms for that. Is there any stronger motive?

Said puts his hands over Dov's hands. After a moment, he slowly but firmly removes Dov's hands. Before Dov continues, he regards his own hands, as though they are now strange to him. And this strangeness angers him.

Said Are you done?

Dov No. You're weak. All of you. Bound by chains of backwardness, of paralysis and . . . Don't tell me you spent twenty years crying. To hell with that. Tears won't bring back the missing or the lost, they won't win a battle either. No. All the tears in the world won't carry even a small boat holding two parents searching for their lost child.

Said (*quietly*) How dare you.

Dov You spent two decades crying and whining?! So that's what you're telling me now? Is this your pathetic, worn-out weapon?

Safiyya I don't understand, Said?

Said Yes you do. He says we're cowards.

Safiyya looks at Dov for a beat, and as she speaks she does not take her eyes off of him.

69

Safiyya And because we're cowards, he can become like this?

Said (*to Dov*) My wife asks, if it is true that we're cowards, does that give you the right to be this way?

Dov shakes his head in exasperation and looks away from Safiyya.

As you can see, she's willing to recognise that we were weak. And paralysed. From that standpoint perhaps you are correct. But that doesn't justify anything. Two wrongs don't make a right.

Miriam Nobody is saying that –

Said Oh, but your son is. (*To Dov.*) What about what happened to Iphrat and Miriam? And the people in Auschwitz or the other camps? Because they died or lost everything does that make them cowards too? And if so, does that make it right?

Dov Of course not.

Said First you say that our mistakes and our weakness justify your mistakes and your crimes; then you say that one wrong doesn't absolve another. You use the first logic to justify your presence and our absence, and the second to avoid the punishment your actions deserve.

Dov No. That's not what I'm –

Said You can't see it but these equations of yours are worn out and full of cheating.

Dov No.

Said Yes, Dov. And it seems you even enjoy this strange game. All of you. And here you are, once again, trying to fashion a racehorse out of our weakness and mount its back. No, *Dov*, I'm not talking to you assuming that you are an Arab.

70

Dov (*overlapping*) Palestinian?

Said Palestinian.

Dov (*overlapping*) Arab.

Said Because now I know, better than anyone, that man is not just flesh and blood passed down from generation to generation, like a merchant and his client exchanging a can of –

Said and Dov almost finish the sentence together:

Dov *and* **Said** – chopped meat?

For a split second they acknowledge that they've shared the same image. Then it's gone.

Said No. In the end you're a human being, Jewish or whatever the hell you want. But one day you'll realise that the greatest crime any human being can commit is to believe, even for one moment, that the weakness or mistakes of others give him the right to exist at their expense.

Said stands very close to Dov and looks him in the eye.

And you, do you believe we'll continue making mistakes? If we should stop making mistakes one day, what would be left for you then?

Dov looks away. There is silence between them. Said feels as though he can leave now, for everything has come to an end. He calmly turns to Safiyya.

You know what a homeland is, Safiyya? It's where none of this can happen.

Said loses his balance for an instant. Safiyya stabilises him.

Safiyya Are you all right?

Said I was just . . . You know, Khalid, he doesn't know that vase or Halisa or Khaldun. For him, Palestine is something a man would die for. For us it's a search for something buried under the dust of memories. And look what we found.

Safiyya Dust. More dust.

Said Yes . . . We were convinced that a homeland was to be found in the past. For Khaled, it's the future. That is how we differ.

Safiyya approaches Miriam. She takes her hand, almost formally. It is an awkward moment, but Safiyya nods to her, in a gesture of thanks, mother to mother.

Safiyya Madame.

Then she turns to Said.

Said. I want to leave. I want to hear the sea again before we go back.

Said now touches Safiyya's cheek, perhaps tucks a loose strand of her hair back in place.

Said Yes. Let's listen to the sea before we go. (*To Dov and Miriam, calm.*) There are thousands like Khalid who have no need for the tears of old men searching in the depths of defeat. I think perhaps they will make right the mistakes of the world, the mistakes of men like me –

He breaks off.

Yes, Safiyya. We should go.

Miriam Please. You can't leave like this. We haven't talked about it enough. I want you to know that –

Safiyya interrupts Miriam, and speaks directly to her for the first time, quietly, confidently.

Safiyya There is nothing more to say.

Said You know, for you, perhaps the whole thing was just an unfortunate incident. But history isn't like that. When we came here we were resisting it. As we were when we left, but . . . Well, it seems to me, madame, that every Palestinian will pay a price by the end. I know many who've already paid with their daughters and sons. I, too, paid with a son, in a strange way. And perhaps it was only my first instalment.

Now he speaks to both Dov and Miriam.

And the answer is yes. You haven't asked, but yes, you both may stay in our house for the time being. And use our things. It'll take –

Miriam A war.

Said Yes. To settle it all. I figure it will.

Now, for the first time, Safiyya stands directly in front of Dov. They regard one another. She raises her hand and just barely touches him. Then very directly, simply, Safiyya sings a line of the old lullaby to Dov. Dov listens for some moments.

Dov (*to Said*) What is she saying?

Safiyya doesn't take her eyes from Dov. She sings another line of the lullaby, but now she's speaking it, with only a trace of song.

Tell me what she's saying.

Safiyya lightly passes her hand across Dov's face: it is a gesture of goodbye. Now she looks at Said and something passes between them.

Said Goodbye.

Safiyya Yes. It's time.

Safiyya holds out her hand to Said. For a moment Said is motionless. Dov disappears.

Said takes Safiyya's hand, he kisses it. As he does so, there is a tearing sound, but this time more powerfully, an exhalation almost, as though some force has rent the air. The three of them, Said, Safiyya and Miriam, do not feel the tremor directly, but for a moment they all lose a fraction of balance.

Now Young Safiyya and Young Said enter the house, as though it's still theirs. Their happiness is palpable. Young Safiyya is carrying the feathers, and just showing her pregnancy. Young Said is trying to grab the feathers. She ducks away from him. At first, the others don't see them, but at some point, Safiyya and Said do see their younger selves, and for just an instant they acknowledge each other.

Young Said Who says it will be a boy, huh? How can you know?

Young Safiyya We village girls know more than you. Always. Rain or drought, Ford or Fiat . . . boy or girl.

Young Said Kiss me.

She does.

Young Safiyya It's settled then. We'll name him . . . Khaldun. You like it?

Young Said Yes. I do. I like the ring of it.

Young Said *and* **Young Safiyya** Khaldun.

They both laugh at the delight of the name.

Said (*to Safiyya*) I hope Khalid will have gone to the mountains while we were away.

Safiyya Yes.

Said and Safiyya take a last look around the room/ house. This last moment is not nostalgic, but filled with firm choice to leave the past behind. Now Safiyya, Said and Miriam disappear, leaving only the young lovers on stage. Suddenly, there is a sharp, loud crack, like distant thunder, moving closer.

Young Said What's that?

Young Safiyya Let's go look.

Young Safiyya and Young Said run out of the house to see what has made the strange, urgent noise. They glance around, more curious than frightened. Now the noise strikes above them, again. It's a thunderous, rupturing sound. Both beautiful and frightening in its promise.

Said . . . It's coming. Listen.

The youths look up at the noise, with both anxiety and hope, trying to glimpse what's coming.

Can you see it?

Young Said I can see it. It's coming. Yes.

Young Safiyya Yes.

End of play.